Discovering Science
EARTH AND SPACE

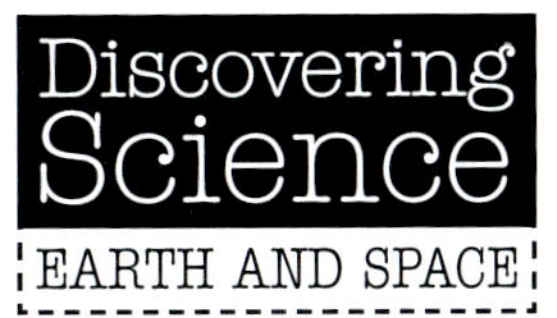

The Weather

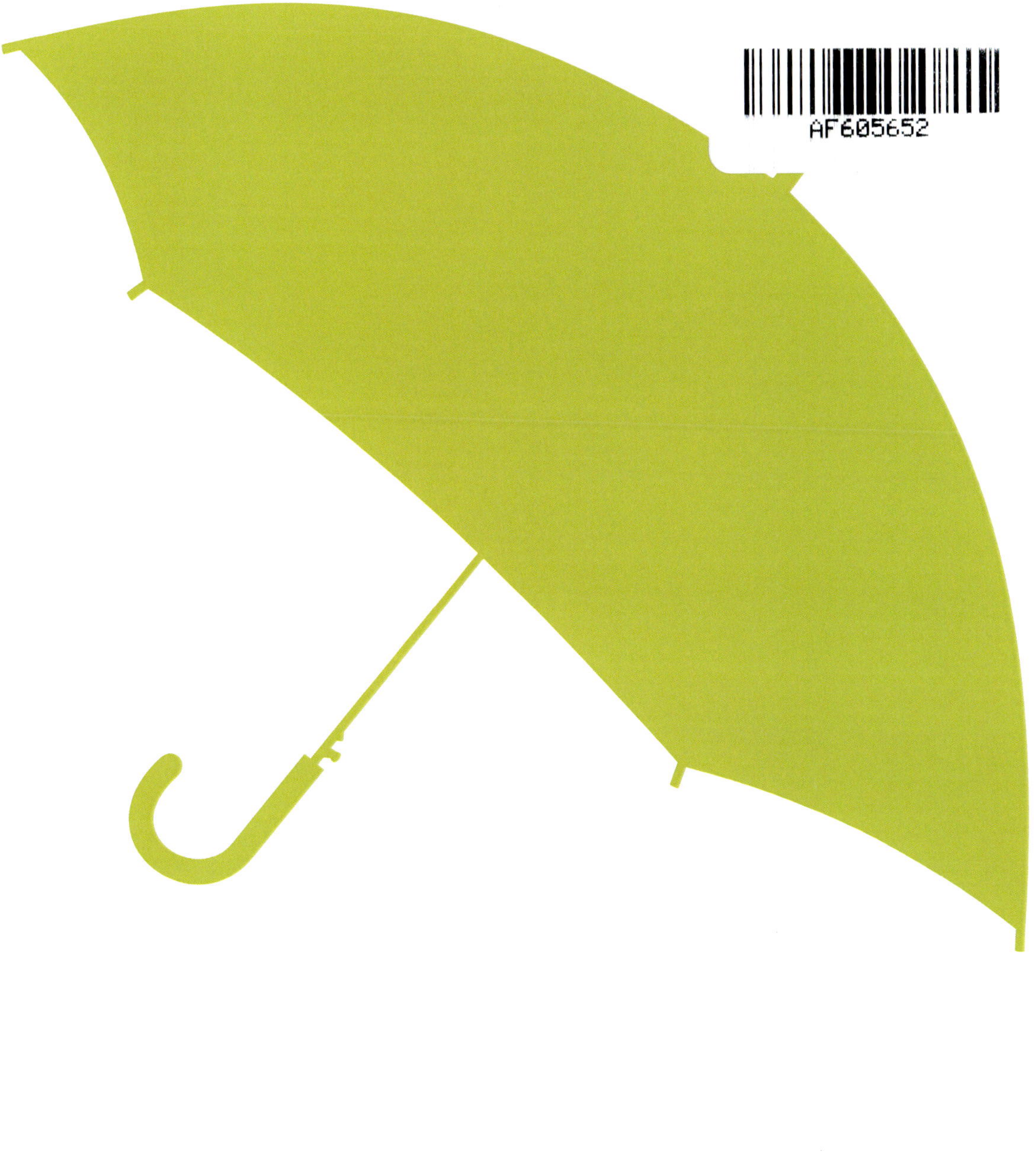

The weather changes every day. On rainy days, you might choose to play inside.

On hot, sunny days, you might go to the beach.

On rainy days, you wear a raincoat and gumboots.

On hot days, you wear a T-shirt, shorts and a hat.

Some places can be very cold. It can be so cold that it snows.

When it snows, people wear jackets, hats and gloves to stay warm.

People who live in really cold places do other things, too. In Japan, children can play in the snow.

Animals are also affected by the weather. Lizards lie out in the sun to warm up.

Birds shelter in trees when it rains.

Animals hide in the shade when it is very hot.

In some places, it gets so cold that animals hide for the whole of winter. This is called hibernating. Bears hibernate.

The weather changes every day.
What is the weather like today?
What are you going to do?